THE AMAZON

GALLERY BOOKS
An Imprint of W. H. Smith Publishers Inc.
112 Madison Avenue
New York City 10016

This edition first published in U.S.
in 1990 by Gallery Books,
an imprint of W.H. Smith Publishers, Inc.
112 Madison Avenue, New York, New York 10016

ISBN 0-8317-9594-8

Printed and bound in Spain

For rights information about the photographs in
this book please contact:

The Image Bank
111 Fifth Avenue, New York, NY 10003

Producer: Solomon M. Skolnick
Writer: Wallace Kaufman
Design Concept: Lesley Ehlers
Designer: Ann-Louise Lipman
Editor: Joan E. Ratajack
Production: Valerie Zars
Photo Researcher: Edward Douglas
Assistant Photo Researcher: Robert V. Hale
Editorial Assistant: Carol Raguso

Title page: **Trees overhanging Brazil's Rio Negro drop seeds and insects into the nutrient-poor water and make it possible for fish to survive.** *Opposite:* **In Peru's Cutibereni National Park, an Amazon tributary carries rich sediments from the Andes Mountains toward the rain forests of Amazonia. This erosion is vital to the life of the lower forests.**

The equator crosses the Atlantic coast of Brazil a few miles north of an island almost as large as Switzerland. Under the year-round glare of the tropical sun, the waters of the Amazon River flow flat and brown around the 15,500 square miles of Marajó Island, the last of many unusual achievements of the greatest river on earth. They pass a million people in the port city of Belém and push out into the ocean, staining it brown offshore for 150 miles. The mouth of the Amazon is 200 miles wide, and beneath the shallow coastal water it has piled its cargoes of mud and silt 12,000 feet deep.

On the other side of South America, only 100 miles from the Pacific Ocean, is a rocky, naked land where freezing winds forbid anything but lichens and tough grasses to grow. The few Quechua Indians who climb the mountain passes wrap themselves in thick wool ponchos and hats. Most visitors gasp for breath in the thin air and take pills to fight altitude sickness. This is the altiplano of the Andes Mountains in Peru. It looks and feels like the arctic tundra.

When the clouds break and the midday sun shines through the thin air, the gleaming snow on the slopes of Mt. Mismi and Mt. Quehuisha melts slowly. Curtains of ice on the gray-black cliffs melt by day and freeze by night. The melt waters run across the barren land in a cobweb of tiny streams. With them they carry silt and minerals from the relatively new and still sharp peaks of the Andes. In this freezing world, 18,363 feet above sea level, begins Amazonia, the world of the Amazon River. The ice water that trickles across the rocks flows 4,200 miles before it reaches the Atlantic Ocean.

Above: **The sharp ridges of the eastern Andes are typical of young and quickly eroding mountains.** *Left:* **Moisture carried west from the Atlantic is blocked by Peru's Andes and is filtered by forests as it heads back toward the ocean.**

In the lowlands of Peru, a river begins to distribute its sediments, its looping path typical of flat country. *Below:* Vegetation colonizes the sandbars of the Rio Negro.

This page: These Queen Victoria water lilies *(Victoria amazonica)* float their huge leaves, drawing energy from the tropical sun and nutrients from the soil-enriched waters. *Opposite:* A short distance from its union with the Amazon, Brazil's Rio Negro floods an island forest in an area called the Archipelago of Anavilhañas.

Above, left to right: **One of many palm species bears its heavy flowers and fruits close to the trunk for good support. The stranglers are plants that start life on the limb of a host tree and drop roots to the forest floor, eventually engulfing the host and killing it.** *Below:* **The leaves of this Amazon lily can be six feet across, providing shelter beneath for a variety of small aquatic animals.**

Between Mt. Mismi and the Atlantic Ocean lies the most important natural area in the world. Its arctic-like beginning and its equatorial end symbolize the Amazon River basin's importance to the world's climate and economy. Amazonia, the world drained by the Amazon River, is almost as large as the entire U.S. Africa's Nile River is longer than the Amazon by only 50 miles. The Amazon, however, carries 60 times as much water as the Nile and 14 times as much as the Mississippi. This gigantic flow carves a channel that is sometimes more than 300 feet deep. It is fed by over 500 tributaries from eight major river systems. Their combined length stretches over 50,000 miles. Ships can travel 2,000 miles inland on the Amazon and still be only 300 feet above sea level, a rise of less than two inches per mile.

On an average day the river pours 7 million cubic feet of water per second into the ocean. For thousands of years this water has also carried over 2,500,000 tons of silt a day to the coast of South America, where the sediment rests in a deposit now over two miles thick. From its 2,700,000-square-mile drainage basin, the Amazon contributes a fifth of all the river water reaching the world's oceans.

The Amazon is said to begin at Mt. Mismi because the water that melts from the snows there travels farther than the water in any other tributary. The Amazon, however,

This page, top to bottom: **The flamingo flower,** *Anthurium,* **attracts pollinators with its brilliant color. One of the many members of the bladderwort family,** *utricularioides* **carries one seed in each of its cascading flowers. A close look at a mimosa flower shows its complex structure.**

The *Masdevallia* orchid is typical of the epiphytes that have adapted to life in the branches of trees. *Below:* Small tree frogs find bromeliads like *neoregelia* often hold enough water between leaves to make a miniature pond.

Ecuador's high forest is graced with many species of orchids. *Below:* Although most of Amazonia is blanketed with various shades of green, the forest does contain patches of dazzling color. *Overleaf:* The scarlet passionflower vine *(Passiflora coccinea)* grows across the breadth of Amazonia.

really has thousands of beginnings in mountains from Venezuela's 8,400-foot Mount Marahuaca north of the equator to Bolivia's 20,201-foot-high Illimani, 1,100 miles south of the equator. For the length of South America these mountains form a wall that blocks the warm, moist Atlantic air masses, forcing them to drop their rains in Amazonia.

The lush, green jungle life that most people associate with the Amazon valley begins in the brilliant snows and dark stones of the high Andes. The little streams that drip from the snow-covered peaks quickly form small rivers. They cut their way downhill carrying boulders and pebbles. 4,000 feet below the summit of Mt. Mismi, in a land still too hostile for trees, the cold, green-white waters join in the Hornillos River. Soon other streams join and form the Apurímac River, a flow strong enough to cut deep valleys in the stone.

The Apurímac carves some of the world's deepest gorges as it drops over 13,000 feet in 300 miles. For many miles its canyon is over 10,000 feet deep as the water rushes down a steep slope. Here few people use the river except to fish for trout in its quieter places. Several expeditions have been launched to run the river in kayaks, but very few have succeeded.

This harsh country and the powerful rivers high above the green life of the warm Amazon River basin might appear to be an insignificant prelude to the real Amazon valley.

Preceding page: **One type of termite, *Amitermes excellens*, earns its name by its architecture and its ability to quickly recycle deadwood. *This page, top to bottom:* Leaf-cutting *Atta* ants can strip a tree overnight, but instead of eating the leaves they carry, they use them in their nests to grow yeasts and fungi. Carnivorous bees have learned to sustain themselves by eating meat. These bees (*Trogona bypogaea*) begin their meal in the serpent's mouth.**

Several species of tarantulas inhabit Amazonia, but even those that sting seldom do more than irritate a human. This "bird-eating" spider is qui⟨...⟩ and big enough to capture a small bird. *Below: Paraplectana* is a spider whose bright colors advertise its presence.

Above: The harlequin beetle *(Acrocinus longimanus)* takes its common name from the many-colored clothes of a court jester.
Right: The *Scarabacidae* beetle wears its distinctive bright color much like an exotic bird or flower.

Preceding page: While it feasts on a katydid, the leaf-imitating mantis shelters under its protective camouflage. From above, it looks like another leaf in the forest. *This page, right:* A katydid *(Orthoptera tettigoniidae)* molts as it outgrows its external skeleton. *Below:* This katydid disguises itself as a dry leaf but uses its "startle" display to attract attention from other members of its species.

The mountainous headwaters are less than 10% of Amazonia, but most of the load of silt and minerals that the river delivers to the lower forests and the Atlantic Ocean begins here, where the fast, cold waters tear at the steep mountain slopes and grind stone into silt. Almost 96% of the dissolved salts and over 80% of the silts that fertilize the river's flood plain are carried from these mountainous beginnings.

The rain forests along the rivers could not exist without this nourishment. The rocks underlying the Amazon River basin are among the oldest in the world, and most of the nutrients in Amazonia's ancient soils disappeared long ago.

Only a few hundred miles from the snowcapped peaks of the Andes, the mountain rivers have already plunged so far that they have entered a warmer, flatter country and have become jungle rivers. The first European to see the Amazon did not enter it from the Atlantic, but descended from a mountain river in Ecuador. By February 1542, Francisco de Orellano's conquistadores had found little gold and could not find food. Orellano and some 50 men rowed down Ecuador's Napo River during the flood season to seek provisions in warmer areas. Suddenly Orellano's boat came to the end of the Napo, where it joins Peru's Ucayali. The Ucayali meets the Marañón and the two rivers become the Amazon. Here Orellano's boat swept out into the great river, and he

This page, top to bottom: **This coreid bug, a relative of the squash beetle, approaches a meal of plantanillo seeds.** *Umbonia spinosa* **is an appropriate Latin name for this Peruvian insect that mimics a thorn. One of many "stink bugs" which ward off predators by exuding an unpleasant smell, this** *Neodine discocephalidae* **guards its eggs and young.** *Opposite:* **The owl butterfly,** *Caligo,* **may have developed this large eyespot on its wings to imitate the threat of an owl.** *Overleaf:* **A common sight in Amazonia, the** *Catagramma* **belongs to a family that has about 3,000 species.**

This glasswing butterfly *(Cithaerias)* flies on almost invisible wings, a trait found in several related rain forest species. *Below: A Metamorpha elissa* clings to a stalk in the rain forest.

Looking like small leaf cuttings, these yellow butterflies *(Peiridae)* have descended to the edge of a river, probably to feed on minerals in the mud. *Below:* The black witch *(Ascalapha odorata)* exhibits the chaotic wing pattern that blurs its outline and confuses predators.

Above: The skin of poison dart frogs gives off a toxic chemical, but it would not affect these tadpoles riding to a treetop haven where water may have puddled in the leaves of an air plant. *Left:* This poison dart frog *(Dendorbates pumilio)* wears bright colors to warn predators of its toxicity.

thought what many people today still think at their first sight of these great waters in flood. "It came on with such fury and with so great an onrush that it was enough to fill one with the greatest fear to look at it, let alone to go through it...and it was so wide from bank to bank from here on that it seemed as though we were navigating launched out upon a vast sea."

Orellano's group did not have the heart to fight their way back up the current. Seven months later they passed Marajó Island and entered the Atlantic. With them they carried a hearsay story about fierce woman warriors like the Amazons of Greek mythology, giving the river its name.

Orellano wasn't the only conquistador who believed or made up stories of Amazons in the New World. But he was right about something more important: the lands along the rivers of the Amazon valley are, for much of the year, a vast, shallow sea. Amazonia is such a flat world today because millions of years ago when the Andes rose up and blocked the river's westward flow to the Pacific, the dammed waters formed a giant, shallow lake. Some time later, of course, that lake broke through the low hills along the Atlantic and ever since, the river has flowed eastward.

The rivers that join to form the Amazon are divided into three types by color – white, blue, and black. These colors signify not only the origins of the water but also what they contribute to the overall flow.

Above: The blue-legged poison dart frog is as distinct as a flower, and its colors help predators quickly learn that eating this animal can be fatal. This small frog hides in the wet foliage and is not harmful unless eaten. *Right:* The marine toad *(Bufo marinus),* which may grow to be 12 inches long, is the largest toad in South America, as well as one of the most poisonous.

Above: The horned frog *(Ceratophrys ornata)* is almost as wide as it is long, spends much of its time half-buried, and may eat rodents. *Left:* Like so many small animals in this leafy world, the horned frog *(Hemiphractus)* also camouflages itself as a leaf.

Top Chefs Try to Develop Taste for Amazon Fish At Rain-Forest Benefit

By FLORENCE FABRICANT

Tucunaré
A predatory fish highly valued for its delicious flesh.

Martins

FOR the last few years, we've been inundated with rain-forest products, especially fruits and nuts, to highlight the plight of threatened tropical regions. Now, along come fish.

An exotic contingent consisting of tucunaré, filhoté, tambaqui, pescada, piramutaba and dourada were recently flown to this country for a benefit that had two goals: to interest chefs in using the Amazon fish and to alert people that fish, too, are linked to the imperiled ecology of rain forests.

The benefit, in East Hampton, L.I. on Kay LeRoy's rolling lawns, raised money for the Rainforest Alliance, a nonprofit organization based in New York that is dedicated to preserving the world's tropical forests.

About the only fish from the Amazon River most people can name is the voraciously carnivorous piranha, which, although supposedly delectable, was not served at the benefit because it is annoyingly bony. But there were plenty of other choices, as there are 3,000 species of freshwater fish that inhabit the Amazon, a river system that includes a fifth of all the world's river water.

By creating a larger market for the fish, fish farms could be organized in the Amazon region. That would help preserve the rain forest by creating

A fish with bones like spare ribs.

jobs for local people and using, but not overusing, the local resources.

"Deforestation not only destroys the Amazon in Brazil. It also destroyed any parasites that might be present in the fish.

Although initially wary of using frozen fish, the chefs were generally impressed with their taste. One that was served, tambaqui, eats fruits and nuts from trees that become submerged when the Amazon floods. It grows to 70 pounds and has bones like spare ribs and teeth like a horse. "It's like nothing I've ever seen, and I'd use it again," said Charles Palmer, the chef and co-owner of Aureole in Manhattan.

Among the dishes served were Moroccan spiced tambaqui with sweet onion marmalade, filhoté with mango salsa and crispy ginger, and marinated pescada with green papaya and herbs. Alderwood smoked piramutaba with quinoa tasted better than smoked sturgeon.

Leonard Schwartz, chairman of the Rainforest Alliance, admitted that importing the fish to a place surrounded by plenty of fish of its own "was a crazy, wild thing to try to do." The party served not only as a debut for the fish, but raised money for the Amazon Rivers Project, a five-year, $500,000 program designed to help preserve the rain forest by making the Amazon economically productive.

"We are trying to show that by making the fish an important re-

"Deforestation not only destroys the local resources, but it also damages the Amazon flood plain which is the habitat of these fish," said Michael Goulding, a research scientist at the University of Florida in Gainesville who is director of the alliance's Amazon Rivers Project.

Each guest paid $250 to taste the fish and trappings created for them by some of the New York area's best-known chefs, including David Bouley, Gilbert Le Coze, Jean Jacques Rachou, Ed Brown, Charles Palmer, Michel Bourdeaux, David Waltuck, Eric Ripert, Debra Ponzek, André Soltner and Pat Trama. These chefs, who either work in Manhattan or East Hampton, would not normally touch a frozen fish, much less a block of tucunaré or a whole frozen tambaqui.

But freezing the fish was essential because of the hot climate and the remoteness of the fishery, 1,000 miles up the Amazon in Brazil. It also destroyed any parasites that might be present in the fish.

source it makes more sense to maintain the tropical forest than turn it into grazing land," Mr. Goulding said. None of the fish are endangered in this area of the Amazon, he said, but a delicate balance must be maintained.

"These fish have been exported for 30 years, mostly to Europe and Africa," he said. "But developing an American market for them will add to their value and make it more essential to preserve the habitat."

Even chefs like Mr. Bouley, who is accustomed to having halibut and fresh, hand-picked scallops flown to his restaurant from Maine in a matter of hours, had high praise for the firm-textured, flavorful pescada and said he would serve fish like these.

At the benefit, the chefs were busy tasting each others' food. A few were grudging in their praise. "The fish was better than I thought, even though it was frozen," said Mr. Soltner, the chef and owner of Lutèce. "It would have to be fresh before I use it."

encouraging. He added that he was meeting today with Julia Child, who has expressed interest in using the latest techniques, which can bring fresh fish to 60 degrees below zero in just a few hours.

He also hedged his bets by grinding the dourada into mousse, then studding the mousse with salmon, wrapping it in brioche and serving it with watercress sauce, a less effective way to showcase the flavor and texture of the fish than simply sautéing it and serving it with a splash of sherry vinegar on a bed of summer vegetables, as Gilbert Le Coze and Eric Ripert of Le Bernardin did.

"This fish reminds me of pompano," Mr. Le Coze said.

In coming months, New Yorkers may have a chance to judge for themselves.

Pescada
A first-class food species that feeds heavily on small shrimp in the Amazon River and is found only in fresh water.

Martins

Tambaqui
The most important food fish in the Amazon, sometimes reaching over three feet in length, it feeds off fruits and nuts that fall from trees during flood season.

last time he used frozen fish was 30 years ago, was unfamiliar with the latest techniques, which can bring fresh fish to 60 degrees below zero in just a few hours.

Jeffrey Moats, the president of Kapok International, the fish-processing company based in Cleveland that imported the fish for the party, and who is working with the Brazilian Government to better organize the fish-processing industry, began selling the fish to restaurants in Cleveland in March; he said the response was

Michael Goulding

The blue rivers, like the Tapajós, usually come from the south, filtered through sandy soils until their waters are clear and reflect the sky.

The black rivers, like the Rio Negro, flow from the north. These rivers are sometimes called "starvation rivers" because they drain the most nutrient-depleted soils. Their color comes from the acids in the leaves that fall from the forest. The decaying vegetation not only colors and acidifies the water; it also uses up much of the oxygen that might support other forms of life. Despite their color, the black rivers are among the purest waters in the world, in part because they support so little life.

The white waters are actually the color of coffee with cream. They are colored by the minerals and silts torn from the Andes Mountains by the higher tributaries. These are the only rivers that bring new and rich soils to the flood plains. Where the Rio Negro, a black river, joins the white waters of the Amazon, the two remain side by side for over 20 miles before blending.

The richest lands in Amazonia lie close to the major rivers and spend much of the year under water. This is the 24,000 square miles of *varzea,* or flood plain. Throughout Amazonia, the combination of poor soils, high temperatures, and heavy rainfall conspire against life.

In a northern forest where temperatures are often below 77 degrees, soil bacteria turn falling trees and leaves into humus or top soil that gradually builds up. These bacteria make clay soils more porous

This page, top to bottom: **Amazonia's miles of quiet water are an ideal habitat for turtles like these. This tortoise assumes a typical defensive position. The head of the matamata turtle *(Chelus fimbriatus)* appears to be a piece of plant-covered debris as it lies in wait for something to swim by its wide mouth.**

The anaconda *(Eunectes notaeus),* sometimes growing to more than 30 feet long, usually glides on the surface of the water, snatches animals that come to drink, and kills them in its crushing coils, but here it demonstrates its climbing ability. *Below:* The huge fangs and abundant venom of the night-prowling bushmaster *(Lachesis muta)* makes it one of Amazonia's most deadly animals. *Opposite:* The powerful boa constrictor *(Constrictor constrictor)* seldom harms humans, but it is often killed for its skin or exported as a pet.

and help sandy soils hold water. At temperatures above 77 degrees, bacteria are so active that humus deteriorates faster than it can form. The heat also promotes the breakdown of humus into carbon dioxide, ammonia, and other gases. Finally, the heavy rainfall washes away accumulating soil and dissolves the minerals that might otherwise build up and remain available for plants. When the rainy season fills the rivers, they rise over their banks, bringing new soils and minerals. In a good year the floods can deposit over three and a half tons of sediment on an acre of flood plain. Because the forest is so flat, the flood waters reach miles inland, creating a gigantic shallow sea. Along the upper reaches of the Rio Negro, the *varzea* may be fifteen miles wide. Near the mouth of the Amazon it increases to thirty miles. At the delta it is as wide as 125 miles.

How high the waters rise over the *varzea* depends on the location and the lay of the land. The highest areas along the Amazon's tributaries lie under only a few inches of water. Near Manaus, where the Negro enters the Amazon, the water rises over 30 feet and vast stretches of forest stand for months "waist deep" in water. During the floods, large mats of aquatic weeds form on the waters and some grasses survive by detaching their roots from the ground and floating about the forest as grass islands. Fish thrive on the insects, spiders, and larvae that live on and under these floating islands. Between floods, the water leaves behind both permanent and temporary lakes, which fill depressions in the land. These wetlands are temporarily home

to ducks, herons, storks, and other birds who hunt their vast shallows. The variety of wet and dry areas and the richness of the soils make the *varzea* a world of incredible variety.

One reason a nutrient-poor river like the Negro can support fish is because the flood period allows the fish to wander about the forest collecting seeds and insects. If the rain forests of the *varzea* are cut down, however, the food chain is broken. Unfortunately, Brazil's population is growing fast, and the country may turn to the *varzea* for new farmlands, much as the ancient Egyptians ploughed the banks of the Nile.

In this watery world one would expect aquatic animals to be abundant, but their remarkable diversity has amazed even veteran naturalists. Over 100 years ago the naturalist Louis Agassiz of Harvard discovered over 200 distinct species of fish in a small lake near Manaus. Scientists have identified at least 1,300 species in Amazonia. The largest, the giant catfish, or *paraiba*, sometimes reaches 10 feet in length and weighs more than 300 pounds. By contrast, there are only 192 species of fish in all of Europe and only 172 in the Great Lakes of North America.

Some people tell stories of a time before the conquistadores when turtles covered the beaches midway down the Amazon like ants. Turtles are still vital to both native people and to the town markets where thousands are sold for meat. Hunting

Preceding pages, left: **This emerald tree boa (above) holds on with the lower part of its body, the upper half ready to strike.** *Right:* **The emerald tree boa (below) turns from orange to green as it matures to blend with jungle leaves.** *Right:* **The black caiman** *(Melanosuchus niger)* **spends most of its time basking, but its spiked teeth serve well for spearing and holding fish.** *These pages:* **The spectacled caiman** *(Caiman cocrodilius yacare)* **grows to six feet and has been widely hunted for its skin.**

A bill sent to the White House would immediately ban the importation of overharvested birds like the chattering lory ; the Goffin's cockatoo, center, and the Fischer's lovebird, far right.

John Chellman/Animals Animals (left) ; Jacana/Photo Researchers (center and right

Popular Pets, Vulnerable Species   Birds listed for immediate import ban.

Scientific name (Common name)	Legal U.S. imports in 1989	Approximate retail price	Main exporting country
Agapornis fischeri (Fischer's lovebird)	5,182	$29-$39	Tanzania
Amazona oratrix (Yellow-headed amazon)	6,152	$1,000-$1,500	Nicaragua
Amazona viridigenalis (Green-cheeked or Mexican red-headed amazon)	0	$1,000-$1,500	Nicaragua, Mexico
Aratinga auricapilla (Golden-capped conure)	0	$79-$99	Argentina
Brotogeris pyrrhopterus (Gray-cheeked parakeet)	6,385	$29-$49	Peru
Cacatua alba (White or umbrella cockatoo)	4,975	$800-$1,200	Indonesia
Cacatua goffini (Goffin's cockatoo)	5,917	$600-$1,000	Indonesia
Cacatua sulphurea (Lesser sulfur-crested cockatoo)	712	$1,000-$1,500	Indonesia
Lorius garrulus (Chattering lory)	1,100	$79	Indonesia
Cacatua haematuropygia (Red-vented cockatoo)	6	N.A.	Philippines

Sources: Convention on International Trade and Endangered Species; U.S. Fish and Wildlife Service; Pet Industry Joint Advisory Council; New York Zoological Society

Exotic Birds, at Risk in Wild, May Be Banned as Imports to U.S.

By CATHERINE DOLD

CONGRESS has passed a bill that would sharply reduce the number of exotic birds imported to the United States to become pets, including nearly all of the popular parrot species.

Conservationists have sought for a decade to limit the imports on the ground that overharvesting of birds in the wild has decimated some species. Last year 400,000 birds, most of them born in the wild and many of them members of endangered species, were legally imported into this country, making the United States the largest importer of birds. The new bill would soon slash that number by at least half.

Imports of 10 bird species that are in immediate danger of extinction due to heavy international trading would be banned immediately. One year later the ban would extend to several hundred other species. They are considered to be potentially threatened by trade by the Convention on International Trade in Endangered Species, an international treaty that has been signed by 130 countries, including the United States. The new law would also set guidelines under which some banned species could be imported in the future and would establish a program to help exporting countries conserve native species.

The legislation was negotiated by environmental groups, zoo associations, and representatives of the pet industry and bird breeders. It was approved by Congress late in the session with no opposition, and conservationists say they expect President Bush to sign it. A White House official said the Administration supported the bill in principle and it would be carefully reviewed.

"This is landmark legislation in wildlife conservation," said Ginette Hemley, director of wildlife trade monitoring at the World Wildlife Fund, an environmental organization in Washington.

The bill "is a rational way to regulate harvesting of wildlife species," said Marshall Meyers, executive vice president of the Pet Industry Joint Advisory Council, a trade association also based in Washington. "It cannot go on unfettered."

Most U.S. Birds Bred in Captivity

Six to 10 percent of American households now own a pet bird. Most of the birds sold in the United States, including the common canaries and finches, are bred in captivity and will not be affected by the legislation. Some 15 percent of the United States market, however, is made up of exotic imported birds. About 85 percent of

parrot species, are caught in the wild, primarily in Indonesia, Tanzania, Senegal, Argentina and Guyana.

An estimated 6.5 million live birds were imported in the last decade. Twice that number may have been harvested from wild populations, since as many as 60 percent of captured birds are believed to die in transit.

Existing laws have proved powerless to stop the trade, said conservationists. Some species, like the spix's macaw and the Bali myna, have already been reduced to only a handful of birds and are no longer traded because they are so rare. The Fischer's lovebird, one of the species covered by the immediate ban, is now rare throughout most of its range in

---

Bush may sign a bill to exclude species including most popular parrots.

Tanzania. Imports of these species will also be immediately banned: the yellow-headed Amazon, the green-cheeked or Mexican red-headed Amazon, the golden-capped conure, the gray-cheeked parakeet, the white or umbrella cockatoo, the Goffin's cockatoo, the lesser sulfur-crested cockatoo, the chattering lory and the red-vented cockatoo.

The problem is that the exporting nations are not properly carrying out the treaty, said Dr. Donald F. Bruning, chairman and curator of the department of ornithology at the New York Zoological Society. To trade in any species listed under the treaty, an exporting country must issue a permit declaring that the harvest of the birds does not harm the wild population. Many exporting nations do not have the resources necessary to issue scientifically based permits, said Dr. Bruning. Instead they issue quotas, which are then routinely ignored. Shipping birds with falsified documents is also common.

Except in the case of those species considered the most threatened, importing countries are not required to make a similar no-harm finding or issue any permits.

Under the treaty, Dr. Bruning said, "if another country issued a permit, the U.S. had to accept it." To halt the trade of a species, he said, "you have to prove it was decimating the species, and by then, it was heading for extinction."

Dr. Susan Lieberman, a specialist [...] wildlife trade at the

United States Fish and Wildlife Service, said, "We've been accepting everything on face value hoping that it was not detrimental to the species, and knowing it probably was."

Plans for 'a Lot of Scrutiny'

Under the new legislation, the Fish and Wildlife Service will prohibit imports of most species listed under the treaty, regardless of any document issued by an exporting nation.

"What will be allowed is a very reduced trade under a lot of scrutiny," said Ms. Hemley.

Imports of captive-bred exotic species will be allowed, but foreign breeders will have to be certified by the Department of the Interior. It is expected that the legislation will spur new interest in captive breeding as the less expensive supplies of wild-caught birds dry up.

Exporters or other parties will also be allowed to petition the Secretary of the Interior to remove a species from the prohibited list. To gain an exemption, the petitioners would have to prove the wild-caught birds are being "sustainably" harvested, in other words that the removal of those birds will not deplete the population.

"In principle, sustainable harvesting is a good thing," said Dr. Steven R. Beissinger, a professor of wildlife ecology at Yale University. "But it is not easy with some species. It takes a few years of study, especially with a long-lived species like a parrot."

In one of the few studies of sustainable bird harvesting, Dr. Beissinger was able to increase the birth rate of a population of green-rumped parrotlets by making nesting boxes available. Theoretically, those additional birds could be harvested for export. But, he said, there is no proof that sustainable harvesting of birds will work.

In fact, said Dr. Beissinger, "there is no proof that any bird now in the trade is being sustainably harvested." By allowing species not yet on the treaty lists to continue to be traded, he said, "we are assuming sustainability when we have no evidence for it."

Dr. Lieberman said the legislation "won't solve the whole problem, but it's a step in the right direction," adding, "At least we are going to be able to stop and look first, and see if a species is O.K., and we're going to be able to stimulate countries to come up with good management plans."

The smuggling of birds into the United States, which is a particularly serious problem at the Mexican border, is not directly addressed by the legislation. Conservationists speculate that smuggling might increase at first, but will probably drop off once there are fewer legal birds to provide cover.

Preceding page: The powerful bill of the macaw enables it to open tough seeds. Bright colors help members of the species identify each other in the forest's dense foliage. *This page:* The scarlet macaw *(Flora maceo)* is one of the largest of the parrot family and flies in noisy flocks of as many as 20 birds. *Right:* The orange winged Amazon parrot *(Aras amazonica)* is one of many parrots that live on fruits and seeds in the forest. The orange color is barely visible when the bird is at rest.

Above, left to right: A member of the large cotinga family, the little Cock of the Rock *(Rupicola peruviana)* is a fruit and insect eater whose males participate in a communal courting ritual on the forest floor. The long-tailed hermit hummingbird *(Phaetornis suercilioris)* fuels its high-energy flight with nectar from the rain forest's bright flowers. *Below:* The toucan *(Ramphastos cuvieri)* has a bill of honeycombed bone – light, but strong enough to crush tough fruits and large insects.

Above: The spatulalike bill of the roseate spoonbill *(Ajaia ajaja)* has been adapted for sifting food out of the mud in shallow waters. *Right:* The sharp bill of the tiger heron *(Tigrisom lineatum)* enters the water like a spear, picking out amphibians and fish. The bird's feathers have a special powder to protect them from the daily contact with slimy prey.

These pages: Tall legs and a powerful, long beak allow these large jabiru storks (*Jabiru mysteria*) to hunt in deep waters. The jabiru is one of the region's largest and rarest birds.

The giant otter *(Pteronura brasiliensis)* grows to five feet in length and travels in groups fishing. Now, however, it has been hunted almost to extinction. *Below:* The tapir *(tapirus terrestris)* is the largest hoofed animal in the rain forest, a quick runner that is always found near water.

The lowland tapir, like all tapirs, is an ancient form of animal that has survived in South America. *Below:* The keen sense of smell possessed by the white-lipped peccary *(Tyassu pecari)* enables it to find roots and tubers underground.

the turtles, however, interrupts the natural food chain. Their eggs and their tens of thousands of young are an important food source for both birds and the crocodile-like caiman.

This watery world full of trees is a perfect habitat for snakes and other climbing reptiles like the common iguana. The greatest of the snakes is the anaconda, which can reach 35 feet in length and is as much at home in the trees as in the water.

In Amazonia it is no accident that the largest animal of all lives in the river. The manatee grows to 10 feet and weighs over 2,500 pounds. Like the pink dolphin that also inhabits this area, it has been heavily hunted both for its meat and its oil.

The great variety and strangeness of Amazonia's wildlife has been so vividly and often reported in books, magazines, movies, and television, that many people who have never seen the rain forest believe its animals are a fierce, deadly, and constant threat. The greatest dangers are not the piranhas, snakes, or jaguars, but the animals and plants few people ever see. Malaria is always a danger. Tuberculosis strikes one in five residents. In the western Brazilian state of Acre, leprosy thrives. Particularly miserable is Leishmaniasis, which, like malaria, is transmitted by mosquitoes. Luckily, many modern medicines originate with substances isolated from rain forest plants, animals, and fungi.

This page, top to bottom: **The coati mundi (Nasua nasua), a member of the raccoon family, evolved to use its sharp snout for hunting spiders, insects, and grubs at night. The small ears and eyes of the capybara (Hydrochoerus hydrochaeris) are suited to its life of grazing water plants, swimming with only its ears, eyes, and nose above water. The agouti (Dasyprocta) is the size of a large rabbit and can use its powerful hind feet to jump up six feet from a standing start.**

The tamandua *(Tamandua tetradactyla)*, a small anteater, has a tail which enables it to cling to tree limbs while it goes after ants with its snout and claws. *Below:* The giant anteater *(Myrmecophaga tridactyla)* carries its young while hunting for anthills it can penetrate with its long nose and sticky tongue, which uncoils to a length of almost two feet.

This page: Armadillos *(Dasypodidae),* whose giant ancestors once roamed South America, spend their days in their burrows. *Opposite:* Evolution has put the anteater's mouth and nose way up front where they can follow the strong claws that rip apart termite and ant mounds.

The three-toed sloth *(Bradypus infuscatus)* is related to the armadillo and anteater but, except for coming down once a week to defecate, it generally spends its life hanging upside down from tree limbs by its long, strong claws. *Below:* The smaller two-toed sloth *(Choloepus dactylus)* almost never leaves the trees. *Opposite:* The hair of this young sloth will soon be covered with green algae which helps to camouflage the animal in the tree limbs.

Squirrel monkeys *(Simir sciureus)* are small monkeys that travel in bands of 20 to 30, raiding fruit trees—wild and domestic. *Below:* Banding together helps the squirrel monkeys keep watch for predators.

The white-faced capuchin *(Cebus capucinus)* is a small but very alert and intelligent monkey that lives in the higher regions of Amazonia. *Below:* Like all capuchins, the brown capuchins *(cebus albifrons)* have a highly complex social structure.

For example, the six-foot-long pit viper which inhabits Amazonia kills with a venom that lowers the victim's blood pressure. Scientists have studied this venom, which seldom kills humans, and have developed captoprial, which is used to treat high blood pressure and congestive heart failure. Rain forest hunters tipped their blow gun darts in curare, which they extracted from several species of trees. Today, the drug tubocurarine is used as a muscle relaxer. The bark of the flowering, evergreen tree cinchona yields quinine, the first effective drug against malaria. Quinidine, a drug used to control irregular heartbeat, is also a product of this bark. The enormous, unexplored variety of life in Amazonia may well yield un-imagined benefits for humanity.

The variety of life in the water is mirrored on land in both the *varzea* and the terra firma, the lands which do not flood. Because the frigid temperatures of the ice ages never profoundly affected the area, the plants and animals have had millions of years to evolve. And until two or three million years ago, they were isolated from North America because the Central American land bridge did not exist.

Like Australia today, South America was an island for almost 0 million years. But the plants and animals that evolved on this island continent were more varied than Australia's. However, when northern animals were able to cross the land ridge, they made South America both richer and poorer. Many native meat-eating marsupials could not compete with the bears and big cats. The ground sloth, which was as large as an elephant, also disappeared.

Preceding page: The howler monkey *(Alouatta senicolus)* hangs confidently by its prehensile tail, freeing both hands to search for food. A special throat structure allows its cries to be heard for almost two miles. *This page, above:* The bald tip of the black spider monkey's *(Ateles paniscus)* tail has a ridge like a fingerprint for gripping which enables the monkey to be one of the most graceful tree swingers. *Right:* Among the many things yet to be learned about Amazonia's residents is whether this spider monkey is thinking.

Amazonia, nevertheless, remains the world's greatest treasury of plants and animals, but a casual observer standing in a typical rain forest might easily miss the forest for the trees, seeing only green and more green, trunks and more trunks. The mixed forests of eastern North America present perhaps two dozen kinds of trees. Three acres of Amazonian rain forest may support over 400 species of trees. And on any single tree there may be 1,500 kinds of insects and dozens of smaller plants that have learned to live without touching the forest floor.

Most rain forest life, in fact, goes on far above the ground. Plants in Amazonia struggle for light. Trees must grow high into the canopy of the forest to capture sunlight. The tallest grow to 180 feet and support themselves on trunks 14 feet in circumference. Others feature broad leaves that catch as much dim light as possible. Still others have special flexible joints that allow the leaves to turn toward the shifting light.

The air plants, or epiphytes, have learned to live high in the canopy. Their seeds blow through the forest like dust, settling in the forks of branches. Among these aerial dwellers are cacti, peppers, ferns, and orchids. They draw their life from nutrients in the rainwater that runs down their host's branches and trunks. The rain collects nutrients from the hot tree and also absorbs the wastes from the large and small animals that live in the canopy. About

This page, top to bottom: **The large woolly (Lagothrix) travels in groups of up to 50, living mainly on fruits of the higher jungle regions. Only a few dozen golden lion marmosets (Leontideus rosalia), which weigh less than a pound and feed mainly on fruits and insects, are known to exist in the wild. The common marmoset (Callitrix jacchus) comes from a family of highly ornate little monkeys with high-pitched voices.** *Opposite:* **The cotton-topped tamarin (Saguinius oedipus) shows the long hair and bold patterns that distinguish the tamarins.**

25% of the rain never reaches the earth. It is caught and absorbed by the leaves and the many epiphytes. The rest hits so many leaves and branches on the way down that it arrives as a fine spray.

How can all this variety exist in an area whose soils are so poor? The *varzea*, of course, gets new soil every year. But amazingly, the forests of the terre firma survive on land that would be desert in North America. The Amazon rain forest has developed a complete metabolic engine that is an extremely efficient biological recycling system. The high

Although at home in the trees, the cat-sized, red-faced uakari *(Cacajao caluus)* has a short tail (less than seven inches) which makes leaping difficult, since the tail cannot serve as a counterbalance as it does in other monkeys. *Below:* Red-faced uakari usually travel on all fours along tree branches. *Opposite:* The jaguarundi *(Felis yagouaroundi)* looks like a small jaguar without spots.

**Jaguarundis have successfully populated
regions from Texas to Paraguay.**

The margay *(Felis wiedii)*, a small cat similar to an ocelot, is hunted for its beautiful fur. *Below:* Some importers have tried to introduce the little margay as a pet in the U.S., but its wild nature makes it unsuitable for domestication. *Opposite:* The jaguar *(Felis onca)*, the largest cat in Amazonia, is a stealthy night hunter. It often rests and waits for passing prey on branches overhanging game trails. *Overleaf:* The jaguar is the triathlete of big cats—climber, runner, and excellent swimmer—adapted to all Amazonia has to offer.

temperatures and the constant rains nurture a wealth of microorganisms and insects. These in turn quickly break down any fallen leaves. The wide assortment of plants and animals present means that for almost every product of decay and for every form of life, there is a user. Everything is recycled in this closed system.

While a rain forest floor seems clean compared to the carpet of crackling leaves in a northern hardwood forest, the rain forest nevertheless sheds many more of its leaves. Three to four times as much litter falls from a rain forest than from a northern forest. But instead of shedding only in the fall, the rain forest sheds its leaves all the time. And the natural cleanup crew is always at work.

The variety of plants, insects, and microorganisms that makes the rain forest so efficient is also the reason that modern science looks to the forest for new insecticides, drugs, fuels, and foods. Amazonia is still one of the few places in the world where biologists routinely expect to find unstudied and unidentified forms of life.

They also hope to find an answer to the most important question of all about Amazonia: How much of its riches can we use without threatening its very life and its ability to replenish the oxygen we breathe?

Index of Photography

TIB indicates The Image Bank.